EDWARD G. ROBINSON'S WORLD OF ART

A Cass Canfield BOOK

EDWARD G. ROBINSON'S WORLD OF ART

by
Jane Robinson

INTRODUCTION BY LEONARD SPIGELGASS

EPILOGUE BY EDWARD G. ROBINSON

HARPER & ROW, PUBLISHERS
New York, Evanston, San Francisco, London

Production coordinated by Chanticleer Press, Inc., New York
Printed and bound by Amilcare Pizzi, S.p.A., Milan, Italy

FIRST EDITION

STANDARD BOOK NUMBER: 06-013579-4

LIBRARY OF CONGRESS CATALOG CARD NUMBER: 75-160649

Designed by Patricia G. Dunbar

A Gift to My Husband

CONTENTS

A CATALOGUE OF THE COLLECTION

Courbet, Gustave
    Portrait de Madame Bouvaist

Morisot, Berthe
    Avant le théâtre

Sisley, Alfred
    Le Pont de Saint-Cloud

Pissarro, Camille
    Portrait de Georges
    L'Arbre mort
    La Rue Saint-Honoré, effet de soleil, après-midi
    Le Pont Neuf

Monet, Claude
    Les Saules, Vetheuil
    Paysage d'hiver à Vetheuil
    Bassin de nympheas, Giverny

Degas, Edgar
    La Femme au tub

Renoir, Pierre Auguste
    Place de la Trinité, Paris

Redon, Odilon
    Les Barques

Utrillo, Maurice
    Le Maquis à Montmartre

Bonnard, Pierre
    Paris sous la neige—La Place Blanche
    Nature morte aux fruits

SOME NOTES ON A FRIEND

An Introduction by

LEONARD SPIGELGASS

It is difficult to do what I shall try to do: recreate a figure, reconstitute a time, reveal the *angst* and spirit of a man, a man named, by his own choice, Edward G. Robinson. I am indebted to a man named Margolies, who would now be eighty years old, for background about Eddie's early years. One of the stories he'd be bound to tell his friends, perhaps until he bored them, is that he went to public school with the famous movie superstar, Eddie Robinson. Would he remember the day at the Bronx Oval when he was responsible for turning skinny Eddie from athletics to art?

Margolies was a self-confident bully and a hell of a baseball player; and Eddie was small and unable to catch an easy infield pop fly. Athletically, he was a total failure, but he kept trying—the high jump, the fifty-yard dash, the hurdles—and he always came in last. He couldn't even shoot pool. Baseball was his last hope and that last pop fly was his last chance; when he missed it, Margolies screamed at him and beat him up. The Robinson passion for muscles and the big leagues was deflated. Eddie turned to things a man could do alone: you can listen to music alone or look at pictures. You can even plan to save the world alone.

At thirteen, Eddie had been in this country only four years; in Bucharest, he spoke Rumanian, Yiddish, and passable German, but no English. By the time he was bar mitzvahed, that is by the time he was considered an adult in the Judaic community, he spoke unaccented English without the immigrant lilt. His ear functioned perfectly; it would serve him well in later years and he would discover his eye as an instrument, too.

With Margolies having made the decision that he should quit team activities, Eddie turned inward; he went through a period of self-searching. There was in him a need to excel, to externalize his feelings, to be a part of the community. And so he found his voice.

As a first-generation American, he was intensely patriotic. Influenced by the Nast cartoons against Murphy and Tweed, he took to the public platform. And those who knew him later as a liberal will be surprised to learn that the chief social influence in his early life was Arthur Brisbane and that his political hero was William Randolph Hearst. But then, both Hearst and Brisbane, in those days, were part of the radical chic, and they were the chief opponents of Tammany Hall.

Thus Eddie, who had already made a mark as an elocutionist, a debator, and a participant in many declamation contests, turned to the political front. He delivered closely reasoned speeches when Hearst ran for governor against McClellan. So passionate was his devotion to the problems of man that he tried to enroll in a Yeshiva on Henry Street as a preparation for the rabbinate, but he wasn't even thirteen and they turned him down. Luckily. For as he grew older, his desire to be a rabbi decreased as his theological doubts increased, and now he was determined to be an attorney, a public defender of the rights of man. He was prepared to fight all evil, all injustice, all villainy; each new day was a battlefield. The elocutionist , the performer, the actor were beginning to take over, to meet the challenge each day.

He was elected to the Elizabethan Society and had his first bout with Shakespeare. He played Bottom in *A Midsummer Night's Dream* and Sir Toby Belch in *Twelfth Night*. What he wanted to do—and still does—was to play Shylock, and Macbeth, and Lear.

After leaving school, Eddie haunted the Astor Library, reading the lives of the great actors, Mansfield, Booth, Garrick, Henry Irving, and the great plays from Aeschylus to Shaw. He also read books of dramatic criticism. And he would peer from the second balcony of the Empire and the Lyceum and gaze at Broadway and its great performers. He was youth searching for its role in life. It was becoming more and more apparent that Robinson's place was on the stage but, like all artists whose thrust comes from within, he was not satisfied with drama and acting; he was also fascinated by other arts—painting, music, and sculpture. Thus, naturally, he haunted New York's museums and the book stores on the Bowery and Fourth Avenue. In all these places there were postcard reproductions of the great pictures of the world—Rembrandt, Vermeer, El Greco, Rubens, and Goya—ranging in price from a penny to a nickel. He splurged with his quarter allowance; and that was the beginning of the Edward G. Robinson collection.

He was beginning, at CCNY, to pursue his interests in the arts. He was to find great music an important contribution to his cultural life; he sat in the Great Hall with its Gothic chairs, and listened to the sublime organist, Samuel Baldwin, rehearse Buxtehude and Bach. He organized a dramatic club and a literary club at the University Settlement House and turned that famous scene from *The Bells* into a vaudeville skit which he called *The Bells of Conscience*. And he had the nerve to try it out on the Loew's circuit.

The Loew's people had amateur nights, but Eddie would have no part of that; that was for singers, dancers, and comics who could and did get the hook. No, he was interested in more serious things. He was delighted when he discovered that every Thursday afternoon Loew's had tryouts of new dramatic talent to find new actors and attract new audiences. Eddie gathered a company around him and produced his short play *Gladiators* and the famous burgomaster scene from *The Bells*. The Loew's circuit booked the production professionally, and that was the first time there was ever a playbill that read "Edward G. Robinson in...." It became more and more clear that he was to go on the stage—not as a lark, but professionally and forever.

How could he break the news to his parents? An actor? That was not their plan for Eddie. Obviously, they preferred the law or medicine; they shared a fear of the uncertain life of an actor, for they knew it was what Eddie now calls "a chance-cursed profession." Having known insecurity, they wanted security for him. On the other hand, they realized that their son had always been searching and had at last found his way. They didn't like his way but, with great reluctance, they gave in.

Eddie undertook his career with great caution. At CCNY there was a professor named Adolph Werner, an aged and wise man with much sympathy for young people. Eddie consulted him, and Werner, more sophisticated than Eddie's parents and recognizing, too, the creative needs of the young college student, felt that Eddie should try the stage and receive professional training. Luckily, Werner knew Benjamin F. Roeder, general manager for David Belasco and a member of the board of the American Academy of Dramatic Arts. And Roeder, not entirely convinced that this small, dark young man was exactly the type to be an actor in a world where profiles and height were the style, nevertheless introduced Eddie to Franklin H. Sargent, head of the American Academy. Sargent gave Eddie an audition; from that audition Eddie received a scholarship. It was an audacious thing for Sargent to do and a courageous one for Eddie; he knew that no one was impressed with him. He did not have the classic face of a Barrymore. Although he lacked "face value," he had "stage value," and deep in him he knew he could deliver.

Upon graduation from the Academy, he started on his career. The usual route consisted of three phases, stock actor, road actor, Broadway actor. Eddie followed this course. At the Academy, Eddie had learned that acting is not just strutting. On the professional stage he learned something that was to be of value the rest of his life: If the actor is not interesting, what he projects is shallow and the audience does not become involved. In stock, he played a small part in a road company of *Kismet* and, in 1915, this got him the credentials to seek his first job on Broadway in a play by Roi Cooper Megrue called *Under Fire*.

When one considers the number of young actors trying out for a role in *Under Fire*, it is a wonder that Eddie got the job. The reason was that, in his passion for education, he had devoted himself not only to the arts but to academic studies as well, chiefly languages. It was his knowledge of languages that got him into *Under Fire*—his knowledge of French and German and his certain ear—because the play required that he take four parts, a Belgian, a Frenchman, a Cockney, and a Prussian.

Under Fire was his first Broadway play. There followed forty others in which, little by little, he was noticed, featured, and starred. He was then invited to join the Theatre Guild in a repertory company which included Helen Westley, the Lunts, Claire Eames, Margolo Gillmore, Earl Larrimore, Henry Travers, and Dudley Digges. He played major roles in such diverse plays as *The Brothers Karamazov, Goat Song,* and *Juarez and Maximilian*. His name blazed in electric lights in *The Racket* and *The Kibitzer,* which he coauthored.

Now he had an extra dollar; but no savings banks for him, no thriftiness; instead, extravagance. He didn't spend his earnings on cars; what he did was to start buying paintings by Blakelock, Gilbert Stuart, Wyant, and Twachtman.

His voice and his face had become famous, so famous that Irving Thalberg offered him a million dollars on a five-year contract—five years of bondage to M.G.M. I remember Eddie saying that he turned it down, walked out of Thalberg's office, and was sick. But the siren call of Warner Brothers was not to be denied; he agreed to do *Little Caesar*. When he came back to New York after *Little*

Caesar everybody knew him and he was imitated in every night club in the country.

However, he refused to be just a movie star and play gangsters; he was an actor in the great tradition and so, disregarding the autograph hunters and the fan-magazine syndrome, he acted in a highly intellectual French play, *Le Marchand de Paris,* adapted by Winthrop Ames and produced by George C. Tyler at the Little Theatre. The reviews were ecstatic and Edward G. Robinson was hailed. But on the second night he peered out at the very small house and saw that only forty or fifty people were there. He stood upon the stage and said grimly to himself: "Who in hell am I true to? Nobody's true to me."

It was sad disillusion, one that led him to accept Jack Warner's offer at a fabulous sum, and when he signed the contract he was really sick, for now he was divorced, divorced from the theatre which he loved and to which he had sworn always to be faithful. Being under contract to the Brothers Warner made it vital for him to concentrate all his energies on the movies. And that's what Eddie did.

There are those who insist that Eddie was difficult and temperamental at this time, but it is my opinion that he was a perfectionist, introverted and certain of his own gifts. I can speak with some authority and personal experience as an observer of the trained and dedicated proscenium actor trying to make adjustments to the cameras and the mike. Few ever have done it. Accustomed to the large gesture, the need to project, the immediacy of the role, and the instant audience response, most great actors are unable to adapt themselves. For they have to learn how to "miniaturize," to learn to be effective in small bits, in large close-ups on pieces of film, frequently shot out of continuity.

It takes high technique to master the transfer from stage to screen, to do *Dr. Erlich's Magic Bullet, A Dispatch from Reuters, Five Star Final, A Slight Case of Murder, The Sea Wolf, The Woman in the Window, House of Strangers, The Cincinnati Kid* and then to return to the stage and act in *Middle of the Night* and *Darkness at Noon,* and to achieve success in both media. They require two totally different kinds of talent.

When you discuss acting with Edward G., he frequently uses the phrase, "dramatic intelligence"; he means that, whatever the medium—the theatre, the movies, radio, or television—some inner instinct enables the actor to think of the whole play, the "character that exists in all of us." That is the way to attain magic in a part.

Endless tracts have been written on the art of acting but no one but the actor himself can ever know the deep personality conflict involved in being yourself and somebody else at the same time. If you ask Eddie about this he will tell you that the actor can only communicate if he is deeply interested in the character he is playing. Eddie apparently seemed difficult to the Warner Brothers bosses, demanding that the pictures be made in continuity as much as possible, going over scripts for nuance, subtlety, clarity, and preciseness of motive and stance. To play in film or on stage Eddie had first to know who he was playing, then feel him, then *be* him.

On one of his trips abroad, Eddie was taken by Matisse, *fils,* to visit Matisse, *père,* at the master's atelier in Paris on his seventieth birthday. Eddie exclaimed, "I can't believe it, your eyes are sparkling, you're so alive. What keeps you so young?" Matisse looked at him sternly, "Every day I've got to get hold of something by the throat and strangle it. That keeps me young." Eddie knew precisely what that meant, for Matisse, in summing up his life, had summed up Eddie's ambition. He noted that the master's easel held an extremely stylized still life—utterly unrealistic. And he noticed that on the table next to the easel there was a series of sketches. The first was realistic and photographic; the second a little less so. By the fifth, Matisse had begun to peel away reality and find the essence of the fruit he was painting.

Eddie realized that painting and acting had much in common. You begin with the external appearance and then strip away the layers to get to the essential core. This is reality and that is how an artist achieves truth. While you are being somebody else, in playing a part, you are, at the same time, being yourself.

For some men, in the 1930's, it was easy to disregard the world; you could ignore the Depression and Hitler and buy stocks and real estate at bargain prices. Or you could involve yourself with the Okies and the anti-Fascists and find surcease not only in work but in buying pictures. That's what Eddie did.

He told me once that the need for art comes at an advanced age, after the acquisition of material things and after success. But I doubt whether he meant that; his need for art was earlier, was inborn. His purchase of art came with success. When I asked him why he bought pictures, he said, characteristically, "Because I had a house and a lot of bare walls."

He bought Monets, Degases, and Pissarros. They were, he insisted, far beyond his means; they cost as much as the house. Later, he bought a Gauguin that cost more than the house. In today's market these paintings would fetch astronomical prices. He realized that it was a home he was living in, not a museum, and that began to shape his taste. He started out with two or three good paintings and kept adding others. If one does that, one ends up with very few bad ones. Pictures have a habit of rejecting other pictures they cannot live with.

I asked Edward G. how he knew when a picture was good. He replied that one must be secure in one's own judgment and preferences. It is a matter of being exposed to fine painters and learning their ways and their style; one must appraise their work in their own terms. Then one knows whether a painting is good, middling, or bad. He went on to observe that no performer or artist is always at his best. This unevenness in performance must be recognized and acted upon. And that requires courage—courage enough to be able to imagine saying to M. Renoir, "This painting is not up to your standard; I'm sorry, M. Renoir, it is not up to the standard of a Renoir."

One afternoon, sitting in Eddie's garden, I told him that an art expert had said that the pictures in his collection were "unhappy" in the main, brooding, introverted, and sad. He looked at me sternly. "There is," he said, "no such thing as a happy or unhappy picture. Look at it from another point of view, that of the theatre. Is *The Lower Depths* unhappy? No, because it concerns itself with mankind; and to probe into the problems of man is not unhappy. The probing is what happily sets man apart." He then took a sip of Coca-Cola and used his glass to gesture: "Unhappy pictures are shallow pictures—pretentious, false, ugly. Unhappiness is not to be confused with somberness."

Just as no picture he has bought has lost its power to move him, so his commitment to the solution of the problems of minority groups, his passion for peace, have lost no steam. Although Edward G. Robinson could be called part of the Establishment, he finds no contradiction in attacking it. He's an agnostic humanist who has turned from a rejection of the religious principle to a respect for it, a nonpracticing Jew, who is Jewish in his soul and whose dedication to humanity is total. He is a radical when it comes to the deprived, a conservative when it comes to the family—a series of contradictions which are, nevertheless, basically consistent.

It is the creative process which interests him primarily; he is unimpressed by changes in fashion and taste. Eddie is a remarkable individual, a small man with a black-and-white beard and brown eyes and a smile that lights up his face, rarely but luminously. He will suddenly display a vast knowledge about a great variety of subjects. Whether he is talking about the Greeks, the Jews, the Boston Tea Party, the Lunts, Sarah Bernhardt, Adlai Stevenson, Malcolm X, Nixon, or Chagall, he speaks with authority.

Some years ago Eddie and Chagall were sitting in Rome, having breakfast, and enthusiastically talking Yiddish as they dunked their rolls in the coffee. A waiter brought them the English papers and Edward G. noted that a Chagall painting had been sold at Parke-Bernet for a record price of $72,000. He mentioned this to Chagall, whose comment was half-Yiddish, half-English. "*Eppis* a snob." *Eppis*, with one shrug, means a positive; with another, a negative. Which shrug Chagall shrugged is the question. As they talked, Chagall observed that prices meant nothing to him, as they mean nothing to Eddie. He added, again in Yiddish, "Who cares? I just keep on *kratzing*" (scratching).

That goes for Eddie, too. He buys pictures, makes movies all over the world, travels up and down this country making speeches for the Boy Scouts, Israel, veterans' organizations, or an occasional candidate. He comes back to his home in Beverly Hills to see his friends and to vote; he smokes his cigars and worries about the world. He reads everything, paints, plays gin rummy, and is one of the world's great hosts. Should you ask him what he is doing, he might well reply, like his friend Chagall, "I keep on *kratzing*."

FROM THE COLLECTION

Gustave Courbet (1819-1877)

Courbet, the master of realism, may be seen as both the last of the great painters in the Renaissance tradition and the first of the revolutionary moderns who dared to fly in the face of convention. He was controversial and daring in his political commitments as well as his art.
Courbet's sensitive portraits of the 1860's are a subdued counterpoint to the rugged landscapes and heroic narrative works for which he is so well known. When he died in Switzerland in 1877, a political exile, Courbet's influence on the younger generation of painters was universally acknowledged and today his works still have a validity and meaning far greater than those of all but a handful of his contemporaries.

PORTRAIT DE MADAME BOUVAIST

Signed and dated 1864   36¼ x 28¾ inches
Oil on panel   92 x 73 cms

PROVENANCE
Mme. Madeleine Doria, Paris
Galerie Durand-Ruel, Paris
Justin Thannhauser, New York

11

Berthe Morisot (1841-1895)

Within the Impressionist movement, two women were to emerge as significant figures: Mary Cassatt and Berthe Morisot. Berthe Morisot is less well-known today than her American-born associate, but her contribution to Impressionism was an important one. She not only took an active part in the exhibitions of the group as it struggled to achieve recognition, she was also married to Eugène Manet, younger brother of Edouard Manet, and thus served to link the great forerunner of Impressionism with her younger contemporaries. Berthe Morisot's paintings—almost always depicting scenes of family life—have an intimate quality and a feminine charm which set them apart and have endeared them to generations of Impressionist collectors.

AVANT LE THEATRE (BEFORE THE THEATRE)

Signed   22¼ x 12¼ inches
Oil on canvas   56.5 x 31 cms
Painted circa 1875

PROVENANCE
Portier, Paris
Oscar Schmitz, Dresden

EXHIBITIONS
Paris, Galerie Boussod et Valadon, *Exposition Particulière,* 1892, no. 6.
Paris, Galerie Boussod et Valadon, *Exposition Particulière,* 1896, no. 66.
Paris, Galerie Durand-Ruel, *Berthe Morisot, Exposition Commemorative,* 1896, no. 66.
New York, Museum of Modern Art, *Forty Paintings from the Edward G. Robinson Collection,* 1953, no. 19.
New York, Wildenstein & Co., *Berthe Morisot,* 1960, no. 14, illus. in cat.

LITERATURE
Elizabeth Mongan, *Berthe Morisot,* 1960 (Painting Supplement, illus. and titled "Lady in Evening Dress").
M. L. Bataille and G. Wildenstein, *Berthe Morisot,* 1961, no. 59. illus. pl. 28.

Alfred Sisley (1839-1899)

The only Impressionist of English descent, Alfred Sisley was one of the original members of the group and remained one of its most faithful adherents. Virtually always painting in the pure landscape tradition, Sisley never ceased to delight in recording the effects of light on the countryside of England and the environs of Paris. He was never rewarded by financial success in his own lifetime but in the years since his death the purity and subtlety of Sisley's creative expression have ensured him recognition as an important figure in the history of nineteenth-century painting.

LE PONT DE SAINT-CLOUD (THE BRIDGE AT SAINT-CLOUD)

Signed   20 x 24¼ inches
Oil on canvas   50 x 61 cms
Painted in 1877

PROVENANCE
Emil Staub-Terliden, Männedorf
Wildenstein & Co., Paris and New York

EXHIBITIONS
Paris, Galerie des Beaux-Arts, 1937, no. 112.
New York, Museum of Modern Art, *Forty Paintings from the Edward G. Robinson Collection*, 1953, no. 32.
Los Angeles County Museum; and the San Francisco, California, Palace of the Legion of Honor, *The Gladys Lloyd Robinson and Edward G. Robinson Collection*, 1956–57, no. 62, illus. in cat.
New York, Wildenstein & Co., *Alfred Sisley*, 1966, illus. no. 32.

LITERATURE
François Daulte, *Connaissance des Arts*, 1957, no. 56, p. 51 illus.
François Daulte, *Alfred Sisley*, 1959, no. 255, illus.

15

Camille Pissarro (1830-1903)

Born in St. Thomas, Virgin Islands, Pissarro arrived in Paris in 1855 and almost immediately fell under the influence of Corot and the Barbizon School. In the ensuing years his style gradually developed along lines parallel with those of Monet and Sisley, and in 1874 he took part in the first Impressionist group exhibition. Throughout his long career, Pissarro never ceased to experiment, for he was always receptive to new ideas, younger artists, and more daring theories. The bustling thoroughfares of Paris, the quiet charms of the countryside, and the activities of his own family surroundings were all themes used by Pissarro in his constant search for the most effective way of capturing in paint the play of light on nature.

PORTRAIT DE GEORGES
(PORTRAIT OF THE ARTIST'S SON, GEORGES)

Signed and dated 1879   18 x 15 inches
Oil on canvas   48 x 38 cms

NOTE
The traditional title of this painting, as listed in the Pissarro-Venturi Catalogue, is *Portrait de Georges à Cinq Ans*. However, Georges Pissarro was born on November 22, 1871, and would have been seven years old, not five, at the time this painting was executed.

PROVENANCE
Ambroise Vollard, Paris

EXHIBITIONS
London, Alex Reid and Lefevre Gallery, *Pissarro and Sisley,* January, 1937, no. 9.
New York, Museum of Modern Art, *Forty Paintings from the Edward G. Robinson Collection,* 1953, no. 21 in cat.

LITERATURE
Ludovic-Rodo Pissarro and Lionello Venturi, *Camille Pissarro, Son Art—Son Oeuvre,* 1939, p. 147, no. 470, illus.

16

17

Camille Pissarro

L'ARBRE MORT (THE DEAD TREE)

Signed and dated 1880   21½ x 25¾ inches
Oil on canvas   55 x 65.5 cms

NOTE
Compare the version of this painting entitled *La Gardeuse d'Oies a Montfoucault* (signed and dated 1875) which is reproduced in Ludovic-Rodo Pissarro et Lionello Venturi, *Camille Pissarro, Son Art–Son Oeuvre*, plate 65, no. 321.

PROVENANCE
Eugene Blot, Paris
M. Urion, Paris (sold Paris, May 17, 1927, Lot 86)
Galerie Georges Petit
Madame Morin Benezit, Paris
Raphael Gerard, Paris
Lefevre Galleries, London
M. Goldman, New York, 1933
J. Furst, London, 1936

EXHIBITIONS
New York, Museum of Modern Art, Los Angeles County Museum; and the San Francisco, California, Palace of the
    Legion of Honor, *The Gladys Lloyd Robinson and Edward G. Robinson Collection*, 1956–57, no. 40, illus. in cat.

19

Camille Pissarro

LA RUE SAINT-HONORE, EFFET DE SOLEIL, APRES-MIDI (THE RUE SAINT-HONORE IN THE AFTERNOON SUNLIGHT)

Signed and dated '98   25¼ x 21 inches
Oil on canvas   64 x 53 cms

NOTE
Toward the end of 1897, shortly after the death of his young son Felix, Pissarro apparently felt that work was the only distraction and decided to undertake a new "series." Those were extremely trying days, for he not only mourned a cherished child but was worried about the health of Lucien, who had been seriously ill, and—if this was not enough—there was also the Dreyfus affair whose ugly implications did not fail to concern him. Yet it was almost with cheerfulness that in December of that year he informed Lucien, "I found a room in the Grand Hotel du Louvre with a superb view of the Avenue de L'Opéra and the corner of the Place du Palais Royal (Theatre Français)! It is very beautiful to paint! Perhaps it is not really aesthetic, but I am delighted to be able to try to do these Parisian streets which people usually call ugly, but which are so silvery, so luminous, and so vital. They are altogether different from the boulevards. This is completely modern! My show will be in April." (From John Rewald, *Camille Pissarro*, p. 150.)

EXHIBITIONS
Paris, Galerie Durand-Ruel, *Camille Pissarro*, 1898, no. 22.
Los Angeles County Museum; and the San Francisco, California, Palace of the Legion of Honor, *The Gladys Lloyd Robinson and Edward G. Robinson Collection*, 1956–57, no. 42, illus. in cat.

LITERATURE
Ludovic-Rodo Pissarro and Lionello Venturi, *Camille Pissarro, Son Art—Son Oeuvre*, 1939, no. 1021, illus. pl. 204.
See John Rewald, *Camille Pissarro*, 1963, pp. 44, 150.

21

Camille Pissarro

LE PONT NEUF

Signed and dated 1902   25¾ x 32 inches
Oil on canvas   65.5 x 81 cms

NOTE

Fired by the magnitude and beauty of his subjects, Pissarro infused his views from le Pont Neuf with such delicacy and liveliness, such a superb mixture of intimate observation and broad execution, that they found grace even before his critical eyes. "These pictures are the best I have made," he admitted. (From John Rewald, *Camille Pissarro,* p. 154.)

PROVENANCE

M. A. Bergaud, Sale Paris 1–2 March, 1920, no. 50, illus. in cat.
Wildenstein & Co., Paris and New York

EXHIBITIONS

Paris, Galerie Durand-Ruel, *L'Oeuvre de Camille Pissarro,* 1904, no. 125.
New York, Museum of Modern Art, *Forty Paintings from the Edward G. Robinson Collection,* 1953, no. 23 in cat.
Los Angeles County Museum; and the San Francisco, California, Palace of the Legion of Honor, *The Gladys Lloyd Robinson and Edward G. Robinson Collection,* 1956–57, no. 43 in cat.

LITERATURE

Ludovic-Rodo Pissarro and Lionello Venturi, *Camille Pissarro, Son Art—Son Oeuvre,* 1939, no. 1213, illus. pl. 238.
See John Rewald, *Camille Pissarro,* 1963, pp. 45, 154.

23

Claude Monet (1840-1926)

In 1874, a group of young Parisian artists held their first joint exhibition at the gallery of a photographer named Nadar. One of the participants, Claude Monet, showed a painting entitled Sunrise —An Impression, *and — prophetically enough—a hostile critic seized upon the title and dubbed the whole group "Impressionists," a term which, for many years, would be used only in derision by the entire French art establishment. Influenced originally by Boudin and Jongkind, Monet was the leading figure of Impressionism and he was always to remain faithful to the concepts and practices of this movement he had helped to create. Of particular interest is Monet's treatment of certain themes such as haystacks, poplars, Rouen Cathedral, or his beloved water lily pond at Giverney in a series of paintings done at different times of the day and under varying weather conditions. Surely it is impossible to overestimate Monet's influence and importance and one cannot help but concur in Cézanne's rebuttal to a dismissal of Monet as being merely "an eye":* "He is only an eye, but what an eye!"

LES SAULES, VETHEUIL (WILLOWS AT VETHEUIL)

Signed and dated 1880   23½ x 29½ inches
Oil on canvas   59.5 x 75 cms

EXHIBITIONS
New York, Museum of Modern Art, *Forty Paintings from the Edward G. Robinson Collection,* 1953, no. 18 in cat.

Claude Monet

PAYSAGE D'HIVER A VETHEUIL
(VETHEUIL IN WINTER)

Signed and dated '86   26¼ x 32¼ inches
Oil on canvas   66.5 x 82 cms

PROVENANCE
Edward G. Robinson, Beverly Hills
M. Knoedler & Co., Inc., New York
Stavros Niarchos, Paris

EXHIBITIONS
Los Angeles County Museum; and the San Francisco, California, Palace of the Legion of Honor, *The Gladys Lloyd
   Robinson and Edward G. Robinson Collection,* 1956–57, no. 34, illus. in cat.

27

Claude Monet

BASSIN DE NYMPHEAS, GIVERNY
(THE WATER LILY GARDEN, GIVERNY)

| Signed | 54½ x 58¾ inches |
| Oil on canvas | 138.5 x 149 cms |

NOTE

After finishing his London series, Monet took up the subject of his water garden once more. This time, however, he turned his attention to the water lilies and to the design created on the surface of the water around them by reflections of the trees and sky with the consequent play of light. Here Monet found a subject which was to preoccupy him until the end of his life. The *Nympheas* was to prove the most difficult of any series that he had attempted, not least, one may suppose, because as he went on working his sight was progressively failing. This explains why the brushwork becomes increasingly broad and the design much looser as the series progresses, the differences in quality of execution between one picture and another, and the fact that so many were left unfinished. Nevertheless, considered as a whole, Monet's *Nympheas* stands out as one of the most lyrical, inventive, and daring groups of paintings in his whole *oeuvre*. According to Daniel Wildenstein, the author of the forthcoming *catalogue raisonné* of Monet's work, this picture was painted circa 1917.

PROVENANCE
Wildenstein & Co., New York
Allard (bought from Monet)
Madame Ozil (daughter of M. Allard)

LITERATURE
Daniel Wildenstein, *Claude Monet-catalogue raisonné* (in preparation).

28

Edgar Degas (1834-1917)

It is ironic that today Edgar Degas, the aloof, aristocratic misogynist, should be most popularly known through his works depicting ballet dancers, laundresses, and women washing themselves in humble surroundings. Degas came from a well-to-do banking family and was never totally dependent on the sale of pictures for his income. Partly for this reason and partly because he was such a perfectionist that he hated to acknowledge the final completion of a work by selling it, comparatively few of his works were acquired during his lifetime. Instead, the bulk of his production was sold at auction after his death. Whether finished and signed (as in the present example) or unfinished and marked with the stamped signature of the vente, Degas's works in all media—but especially pastel—reflect the unique vision and brilliant technique of this lonely and still enigmatic Impressionist.

LA FEMME AU TUB (AFTER THE BATH)

Signed   28¼ x 28 inches
Pastel   71.5 x 71 cms
Executed circa 1891

NOTE

"Degas never surrendered a subject until he had tried it from every available point of view. When he returned to his theme of a woman taking a bath in a round tin tub, he made something entirely different each time. He had the ability to see freshly over and over again. These women, whom he studied so assiduously in the intimate confines of their boudoirs, do not exist as individuals. He seldom personified them; their faces are often hidden by the poses he caught them in; usually there is only a line of cheek, an ear, a slight indication of profile. The artist concentrated instead on the supple or tensed bodies and rendered, by his powerful drawing, the play of muscles beneath their light-struck flesh. There is something curiously chaste about his reaction; his nudes are never voluptuous and they lack the healthy animalism of Rubens or the radiant sensuality of Renoir. They are first and foremost studies of the human form and only secondarily women." (From Daniel Catton Rich, *Degas*, p. 112.)

PROVENANCE
1ère Vente, Degas, Paris, Galerie Georges Petit, May 6–8, 1918, no. 119, illus. in cat.
Jacques Seligman, Paris (sold New York, January 27, 1921, no. 32)
Galerie Durand-Ruel, Paris

EXHIBITIONS
London, Thos. Agnew & Sons, *Exhibition of Pictures, Pastels and Drawings by E. Degas*, illus. p. 635, 1936, no. 6.
New York, Durand-Ruel Galleries, *Degas, An Exhibition for the Benefit of American Aid to France*, 1947, no. 4.
New York, Wildenstein & Co., *Nude in Painting*, 1956, no. 30.

LITERATURE
P. A. Lemoisne, *Degas et Son Oeuvre*, 1943, vol. III, no. 1097.
Arts Magazine, January, 1959, illus. p. 44.
Daniel Catton Rich, *Degas*, 1951, p. 112.
Jean Bouret, *Degas*, 1965, p. 181.

Pierre Auguste Renoir (1841-1919)

Recognized as the greatest Impressionist painter of the nude, Renoir also shared with Pissarro an appreciation of the pictorial possibilities to be found in the Paris of the late nineteenth century. As a boy, Renoir was apprenticed as a painter of flowers in the porcelain factory at Limoges. From this point, throughout his entire career, even in old age when a paintbrush had to be strapped to his crippled hand, Renoir never deviated in his portrayals of the delights of the senses. Whether in a still life, a landscape, or a figure subject, the great traditions of French painting were carried on by this master of Impressionism.

PLACE DE LA TRINITE, PARIS

Signed   25¾ x 21½ inches
Oil on canvas   65.5 x 54.5 cms
Painted circa 1892

PROVENANCE
Ambroise Vollard, Paris

EXHIBITIONS
New York, Knoedler Galleries, *Exhibition of Paintings from the Ambroise Vollard Collection*, 1933, no. 32 in cat.
New York, Knoedler Galleries, *Views of Paris*, 1939, no. 33 in cat.
New York, Museum of Modern Art, *Forty Paintings from the Edward G. Robinson Collection*, 1953, no. 25 in cat.
Los Angeles County Museum; and the San Francisco, California, Palace of the Legion of Honor, *The Gladys Lloyd Robinson and Edward G. Robinson Collection*, 1956–57, no. 46, illus. in cat.

LITERATURE
Ambroise Vollard, *Pierre Auguste Renoir*, 1918, p. 29, illus. pl. 115 (listed as painted in *1895*).
Apollo, November, 1933, illus. p. 340.
Art News, January 14, 1939, illus. p. 8.

33

Odilon Redon (1840-1916)

Although Redon's lifespan almost exactly parallels those of Monet and Renoir, his artistic career and achievements bear little relationship to those of his Impressionist contemporaries. Redon's place is with the Symbolist artists and his fascinating, sometimes frightening treatment of mysterious themes echoes the literary efforts of the Symbolist poets and writers such as Mallarmé, Huysmans, and Flaubert. Incredibly lovely flower pieces alternate, in his oeuvre, with strange creatures and exotic voyagers. Later painters and critics have come to recognize the immense influence of Redon, and any appreciation of the Surrealist movement is difficult without an acknowledgment of his contribution.

LES BARQUES (FISHING BOATS)

Signed   28¾ x 39½ inches
Oil on canvas   73 x 100 cms
Painted circa 1907

PROVENANCE
P-A Regnault (sold, Paul Brant, Amsterdam, 20.10.1958, no. 101, illus.)

EXHIBITIONS
Djakarta, Musee de Batavia, 1936.
Eindhoven, Stedelijk Van Abbe Museum, 1947, no. 69.
The Hague, Gemeentemuseum, 1957, no. 188.

LITERATURE
Klaus Berger, *Odilon Redon,* 1964, p. 197, no. 212.

Maurice Utrillo (1883-1955)

Utrillo, illegitimate son of the painter Suzanne Valadon, occupies a curiously unique place in the history of modern painting. Despite his artistic family background, Utrillo first took up painting only as a form of therapy in combatting his lifelong drinking problem. Neither a "primitive" nor an academic, in the strict sense, his peculiar vision found a rich and varied subject matter in the streets of Montmartre and the buildings of innumerable French villages. The solidity of his forms contrast sharply with the shimmering landscapes of the Impressionists and in some ways are seen to be related to the development of the Cubists.

LE MAQUIS A MONTMARTRE

Signed, titled and dated 1936   20½ x 26 inches
Watercolor   52 x 66 cms

Le Maquis à Montmartre,

Maurice, Utrillo, V.
1926.

37

Pierre Bonnard (1867-1947)

Born in a suburb of Paris, Bonnard ended his life at Le Cannet on the Riviera and the contrast between the two places points up the contrast between the artist's early works—somber, intellectually motivated, urbane—and his later efforts—dazzling sun-filled canvases alive with rich foliage and languorous nudes. Bonnard's first one-man show at the Durand-Ruel Gallery in 1896 was followed by a long association with the Galerie Bernheim-Jeune; the artist's reputation grew slowly but surely throughout Europe and then America (he was awarded the second prize at the Carnegie International Exhibition of 1936—Leon Kroll won first prize). Throughout his career, from the city scenes of the turn of the century, influenced by art nouveau and the Nabi movement, to his last periods, Bonnard's art progressed in a serene, orderly way reflecting a love of nature and humanity refined by taste and a heightened sensual awareness.

PARIS SOUS LA NEIGE—LA PLACE BLANCHE (PARIS IN THE SNOW—PLACE BLANCHE)

Signed   23¾ x 31¼ inches
Oil on paper   60 x 79.5 cms
Painted circa 1901

EXHIBITIONS
New York, Museum of Modern Art, *Forty Paintings from the Edward G. Robinson Collection*, 1953, no. 1.
Los Angeles County Museum; and the San Francisco, California, Palace of the Legion of Honor, *The Gladys Lloyd Robinson and Edward G. Robinson Collection*, 1956-57, no. 1, illus. in cat.
New York, Museum of Modern Art, Chicago Art Institute, and Los Angeles County Museum, *Bonnard and His Environment*, 1964–65, p. 34, illus. in cat.

LITERATURE
Jean and Henry Dauberville, *Bonnard, Catalogue Raisonné de l'Oeuvre Peint*, 1906–19, p. 70, no. 4, illus.

39

Pierre Bonnard

NATURE MORTE AUX FRUITS
(STILL LIFE WITH FRUIT)

Signed   13¾ x 18 inches
Oil on canvas   34.5 x 46 cms
Painted in 1907

EXHIBITIONS
Paris, Galerie Bernheim-Jeune, 1926.
Los Angeles County Museum; and the San Francisco, California, Palace of the Legion of Honor, *The Gladys Lloyd Robinson and Edward G. Robinson Collection*, 1956–57, no. 4, illus. in cat.

LITERATURE
Jean and Henry Dauberville, *Bonnard, Catalogue Raisonné de l'Oeuvre Peint*, 1906–19, 1968, no. 439, illus. p. 70.

Jean Edouard Vuillard (1868-1940)

Vuillard's work first achieved recognition during his association with the group of Parisian symbolist artists known as the Nabis. The group, which included Bonnard, Roussell, and Denis, was greatly influenced by the theories of Gauguin and Serusier who, in contrast to the Impressionists, believed that natural forms had to be interpreted—not merely recorded—in order to create a work of art. Developing his own distinctive style within the movement, Vuillard received valuable encouragement, inspiration, and patronage from the Natanson family; in his intimate small paintings and in his large decorative panels, the artist very often depicted members of this family, amid their circle of writers, painters, and intellectuals, seated in a salon or conversing in a sunlit garden. In Vuillard's best works, the central figures blend with the rich variety of inanimate objects in the background to achieve a mood of intimacy and charm which remains unsurpassed in its appeal to the sophisticated devotee of modern painting.

MADAME VUILLARD A SAINT-HONORE (MADAME VUILLARD BEFORE A WINDOW)

Stamped signature (Lugt no. 2497a)   13¾ x 10¾ inches
Oil on board   35 x 27.5 cms
Painted circa 1895

PROVENANCE
O'Hana Gallery, London

EXHIBITIONS
London, O'Hana Gallery, 1958, illus. in cat.

Jean Edouard Vuillard

DE JEUNER DU MATIN   (THE BREAKFAST TABLE)

Signed   19¼ x 22¾ inches
Oil on board   49 x 58 cms
Painted circa 1902

PROVENANCE
Thadée Natanson, (sold, Paris, June 13, 1908, no. 57, 800 francs)
Paul Vallotton, Lausanne
Joseph Stransky, New York
Wildenstein & Co., Inc., New York

EXHIBITIONS
New York, Galerie Bernheim-Jeune, May 1903.
Los Angeles County Museum; and the San Francisco, California, Palace of the Legion of Honor, *The Gladys Lloyd Robinson and Edward G. Robinson Collection,* 1956–57, no. 71, illus. in cat.
New York, Museum of Modern Art, *Forty Paintings from the Edward G. Robinson Collection,* 1953, no. 39.

LITERATURE
Art News, May 16, 1931, rep. (article by R. Flint).

Jean Edouard Vuillard

DENISE NATANSON ET MARCELLE ARON AU PAVILLON A VILLERVILLE, NORMANDIE

Signed   18¼ x 25½ inches
Oil on board   46.5 x 65 cms

PROVENANCE
Sam Salz, New York

EXHIBITIONS
Paris, Galerie Bernheim-Jeune, Vuillard, 1911, no. 4 in the cat.
Los Angeles County Museum; and the San Francisco, California, Palace of the Legion of Honor, *The Gladys Lloyd Robinson and Edward G. Robinson Collection,* 1956–57, no. 72, illus. in cat.

Jean Edouard Vuillard

NU DEBOUT DANS L'ATELIER
(NUDE MODEL STANDING IN THE STUDIO)

Stamped signature (Lugt no. 2497a)   60½ x 42½ inches
Peinture à la colle, mounted on board   153.5 x 108 cms
Painted circa 1918

PROVENANCE
Ker-Xavier Roussel (Vuillard's brother-in-law)
J. Roussel (his son)
Wildenstein & Co., New York

LITERATURE
V. Raynor, *Arts Magazine,* November, 1964, no. 2, p. 58, illus.

49

Pablo Picasso (b. 1881)

Although he is popularly regarded as the creator of double-headed women and huge, metal sculptures, it is important to recognize Picasso's roots in the somber traditions of Spain and Spanish painting. Pablo Diego José Francisco de Paula Juan Nepomuceno Crispín Crispiano de la Santíssima Trinidad Ruiz Blazco y Picasso was born at Málaga in 1881 and pursued his earliest artistic studies in Catalonia. Even after moving to Paris, Picasso remained very much the Spaniard and his Death of 1901, with its echoes of El Greco's Burial of Count Orgaz, manifests a Spanish fascination with death and its accompanying ceremonies in a manner designed to move the viewer to appreciate the importance of the event and its significance for all humanity, not just the sorrowful mourners grouped around the corpse.

LE MORT (LA MISE AU TOMBEAU) (THE FUNERAL)

Signed   38⅜ x 35⅝ inches
Oil on canvas   100 x 90.2 cms
Painted in 1901

NOTE

In the early spring of 1901, the poet Casagemas, who had accompanied Picasso to Paris, committed suicide. This painting is an allusion to the young painter's sorrow at the loss of his friend. A similar group of figures appears in the lower half of a larger composition known as *L'Enterrement de Casagemas*, now in the Petit Palais, Paris. Two studies for *Le Mort* are recorded in Zervos, one a pencil drawing, the other a watercolor and pencil, now in the collection of Walter P. Chrysler, Jr.

PROVENANCE
Ambroise Vollard, Paris
Pierre Loeb, Paris
Pierre Matisse, New York
Edward G. Robinson, Beverly Hills
Stravros S. Niarchos, Paris

EXHIBITIONS
Paris, Galerie Georges Petit, *Picasso*, 1932, no. 6 (*La Mise au tombeau*).
Zurich, Kunsthaus, *Picasso*, 1932, no. 5.
New York, Jacques Seligman & Co., *Picasso Blue and Rose Periods*, November 2–26, 1936.
Los Angeles County Museum, *The Edward G. Robinson Collection*, 1941.
New York, Museum of Modern Art, (March 3–April 12) and the National Gallery of Art, Washington, D.C.
   (May 10–June 24), *Forty Paintings from the Edward G. Robinson Collection*, 1956–57, no. 37.
Los Angeles County Museum; and the San Francisco, California, Palace of the Legion of Honor, *The Gladys Lloyd*
   Robinson and Edward G. Robinson Collection, 1956–57, no. 37
New York, Knoedler & Co., *Loan Exhibition from the Niarchos Collection*, 1957–58.
Ottawa, The National Gallery of Canada, *Loan Exhibition from the Niarchos Collection*, 1958, no. 38.
London, Tate Gallery, *Picasso*, 1960, no. 8, illus. pl. 2a in cat.
Los Angeles, UCLA Art Galleries, *Bonne Fête Monsieur Picasso*, 1961, no. 2, illus. in cat.

LITERATURE
A. Cirici Pellicer, *Picasso antes de Picasso*, 1946, illus. pl. 63.
Christian Zervos, *Pablo Picasso*, 1957, vol. I, no. 52, illus. p. 24.
Roland Penrose, *Picasso: His Life and Work*, 1962, p. 79.
Pierre Daix et Georges Boudaille; *Picasso 1900–1906, Catalogue raisonné de l'oeuvre peint*, 1966, no. VI.2, illus. p. 193.
André Fermigier and Paul Guinard, *Picasso*, 1967, p. 82, illus.

51

André Derain (1880-1954)

Academism, fauvism, cubism, Negro art, and Impressionism were all movements which had an influence on the art of Derain prior to the First World War. But his service at the front seems to have served as a turning point in the artist's career, for he left the swirling currents of these powerful but often ephemeral currents behind him and synthesized an absolutely mature, individual manner which he steadfastly clung to throughout his life. Strong, superbly handled forms; a sure, though subdued sense of color; and a masterful power to compose these elements on the canvas have all served to maintain Derain's place in the pantheon of modern art's "greats." Derain began as the grand old man of French realism, but throughout his career he always maintained the courage of his convictions with—needless to say—happy results.

PAYSAGE   (L'EGLISE DE VERS)
(LANDSCAPE WITH CHURCH, VERS)

Signed   13¼ x 16½ inches
Oil on canvas   33.5 x 42 cms
Painted circa 1912

52

53

André Derain

PANORAMA (PAYSAGE DE PROVENCE)
(LANDSCAPE IN PROVENCE)

Signed   30½ x 70 inches
Oil on canvas
Painted circa 1930

NOTE
"In what respect Cézanne's great follower André Derain goes beyond him is easy to see; Derain also felt transformation of color to be an evil. He strives to organize his structure in such a way that the painting, though strongly unified, nevertheless shows the greatest possible fidelity to nature, with every object being given its true form and its true color. Light becomes for him a pure means; he guides it as it best supports the creation of form, and subordinates it, whenever possible, to the local color. There is no question here of the aesthetic worth of his austere and mighty art; he is one of the greatest of French painters. Cézanne and Derain will stand in art history, like the masters of the Trecento, as painters of transition, but in a reverse sense. Their solution of the conflict between representation and structure in painting will never result in complete success. Encouraged by their great example Cubism seeks new paths to the solution of this conflict." (From D. H. Kahnweiler in his *Der Weg zum Kubismus,* 1920.)

PROVENANCE
Philip Sandblom, Sweden
Dr. Herman Lindquist, Sweden
Marlborough Fine Art, London

EXHIBITIONS
Stockholm, Liljevachs Konsthalle, from *Cézanne till Picasso,* September, 1954, no. 107 in cat. (as *Panorama*).
Marlborough Galleries, *French Landscapes,* November, 1961, no. 17, illus. in cat. (as *Scène de Rivière*).

LITERATURE
O. G. Carlsund, *French Art in Gothenburg,* 1937, illus. no. 2.

(detail)

Walter Richard Sickert (1860-1942)

While he is usually thought of as the grand old man of twentieth-century English painting, it is difficult to place Sickert within the context of the Impressionist movement. Undoubtedly influenced by Whistler and Degas, he clung to many of the academic values of the English nineteenth-century tradition. As a result, much of his earlier work seems more somber, less liberated, than that of his continental contemporaries. However, his style was ideally suited to his favorite subject matter—the music hall and the more mundane aspects of urban life. Paradoxically, Sickert remained the last "modern" painter to employ studio assistants while at the same time using photography as a starting point of his work. Only in later life did he become interested in more typically Impressionist subject matter and his famous series of Venetian paintings typifies this change.

L'ENNUI (BOREDOM)

Signed and dated 1916   18¼ x 15 inches
Oil on canvas   46.5 x 38 cms

NOTE
In her notes on the artist, Lillian Browse describes the paintings in this series as follows: "Of all Sickert's work, it is to the title *Ennui* that his name is perhaps most firmly linked. I know of five versions of the subject; the largest, the least interesting and unhappily the widest known, is the canvas in the Tate Gallery. In composition this is identical with the Ashmolean version, but it has no decorative pattern on the wall-paper, table-cloth or on the woman's blouse. The surfaces are, on the contrary, unbroken and dull, for Sickert was more at home with canvases of smaller dimensions. The painting reproduced here is the most colorful of all and seems to have been done four or five years after the original version. The outsize tumbler is one of Sickert's few deliberate distortions of scale, another being the even greater distortions of the base in *The Bust of Tom Sayers* which is of the same period. Two very good canvases, without the table or the mantelpiece, belong to H.M. Queen Elizabeth, the Queen Mother, and Sir Michael Culme-Seymour. Another, with part of the table and the glass showing, but with Marie's head cut by the top of the canvas, belongs to Mr. Edward G. Robinson, California. This painting is dedicated to the French painter Asselin and is dated 1916."

PROVENANCE
M. Asselin, Paris
Leger Galleries, Ltd., London

EXHIBITIONS
Los Angeles County Museum; and the San Francisco, California, Palace of the Legion of Honor, *The Gladys Lloyd Robinson and Edward G. Robinson Collection*, 1956–57, no. 61 in cat.

LITERATURE
Lillian Browse, *Sickert*, 1960, p. 78, see p. 77 and no. 71, illus.

Amadeo Modigliani (1884-1920)

There is a tendency to exaggerate Modigliani's position as the archetypal self-destructive Bohemian at the cost of his very real achievement within the context of twentieth-century painting. Of all the artists active in World War I Paris, he combined the abstract values of his Italian predecessors with an intense interest in African sculpture and the achievements of Cézanne. The resulting synthesis, allied with his dispassionate, often bitter, insight is personified by the portraits of his friends, mistresses, and acquaintances of the period.

MONSIEUR CERUSIER

Signed   39½ x 25½ inches
Oil on canvas   100 x 65 cms
Painted circa 1918

PROVENANCE
Docteur Givardin, (sale: Galerie Charpentier, Paris, Dec. 1953, pl. XXV, illus.)
Galerie Paul Petridès, Paris
Arnold Kirkeby Collection (sale: Parke-Bernet, November, 1958, Lot 18, illus. in cat.)

EXHIBITIONS
Paris, Galerie Bing, *Modigliani*, 1927.
Bern, Kunsthalle, *Modigliani, Campigli, Sironi*, 1955, no. 24, illus. in cat.

LITERATURE
Ambrogio Ceroni, *Amadeo Modigliani*, 1958, p. 61, no. 117, illus.

Chaim Soutine (1894-1943)

Born in Smilovitchi, near Minsk, in Lithuania, Soutine escaped from the antiartistic atmosphere of the ghetto to arrive in the heady world of early twentieth-century Paris. The violence of his style often coincided with the subject at hand, as in his twisted landscapes and depictions of decaying carcasses. Sometimes, however, it contrasted with a tender sensitivity toward a gentle, often innocent subject, such as a choirboy, or—in the present example—a communicant. Soutine's temperament must have led him to seek out these calm and pure subjects as an antidote to the violence and torment with which he is usually associated.

LA COMMUNIANTE *(THE COMMUNICANT)*

Signed   32 x 18¾ inches
Oil on canvas   81 x 47.5 cms
Painted circa 1925

NOTE
"Uniforms undoubtedly appealed to Soutine by their unified tonality and less varied textures than 'civilian' garments. And the effect of the uniform is to hide individuality, to de-personalize, to cover uniqueness with anonymity. In Soutine's portraits of costumed figures the uniform serves as a sort of artificial skin, an extension, or analogy, of flesh. He sought to translate both materials into a membrane of oil pigment, for him a sort of protoplasmic source of all things." (Excerpt from Maurice Tuchman's *Chaim Soutine*, 1968, p. 35, in which he refers to pl. 46, *The Communicant*.)

EXHIBITIONS
New York, Museum of Modern Art, *Chaim Soutine*, 1951, no. 46 in cat.
Los Angeles County Museum; and the San Francisco, California, Palace of the Legion of Honor, *The Gladys Lloyd Robinson and Edward G. Robinson Collection*, 1956–57, no. 63 in cat.
Los Angeles County Museum of Art, *Chaim Soutine*, 1968, no. 46 in cat.
New York, Museum of Modern Art, *Forty Paintings from the Edward G. Robinson Collection*, 1953, no. 33 in cat.
London, Tate Gallery, and Edinburgh, National Gallery of Scotland, *Soutine*, 1963, no. 35, illus. in cat., pl. 22.

LITERATURE
Maurice Tuchman, *Chaim Soutine*, 1968, p. 102, pl. 46 (listed as painted circa 1924–25).

André Dunoyer de Segonzac (b. 1884)

The rolling hillsides, rich farmlands, and romantic atmosphere of the south of France have served as fertile sources of subject matter for Segonzac over the decades of his career. He has pursued with steadfast fidelity the depiction in ink and paint of the green field and the lonely village church and today, as curator of the museum at St. Tropez, he is surrounded by his beloved Midi and continues to carry on his love affair with its charm and serenity.

LE CLOCHER DE VILLIERS-SUR-MORIN (THE BELFRY AT VILLIERS-SUR-MORIN)

Signed   28¾ x 36½ inches
Oil on canvas   73 x 92.5 cms
Painted circa 1926–27

PROVENANCE
Galerie Charpentier, Paris

EXHIBITIONS
London, Tate Gallery, 1928
Paris, Galerie Charpentier, 1937
Stockholm, Museum of Stockholm, 1948
Paris, Galerie Charpentier, *Dunoyer de Segonzac,* 1948

63

André Dunoyer de Segonzac

LE CANOTIER AU CHANDAIL ROUGE (OARSMAN IN RED BATHING SUIT)

Signed   19¾ x 25¾ inches
Oil on canvas   50 x 65.5 cms
Painted circa 1924–26

PROVENANCE
Tanner, Zurich
Sam Salz, New York

EXHIBITIONS
Paris, Galerie Bernheim-Jeune, 1925
London, Tooth Gallery, 1932
London, Tate Gallery, 1938

65

André Dunoyer de Segonzac

NATURE MORTE AUX POMMES
(STILL LIFE WITH APPLES)

Signed   25½ x 32 inches
Oil on canvas   65 x 81 cms
Painted in 1928

PROVENANCE
Acquired from the artist
Collection Monteux, Paris
Lord Ivor Spencer-Churchill, London
Galerie Alfred Daber, Paris
Sam Salz, New York
Arnold Kirkeby, (sale: Parke-Bernet, Nov. 19, 1958, no. 14, illus. in cat.)

EXHIBITIONS
London, Tate Gallery, 1936

LITERATURE
Claude Roger-Marx, *Dunoyer de Segonzac*, 1951, illus., pl. 113.

André Dunoyer de Segonzac

VASE D'ANEMONES

Signed	13 x 16¼ inches
Oil on canvas	33 x 41 cms
Painted circa 1935–36	

André Dunoyer de Segonzac

PORTRAIT DE FEMME

Signed   13 x 6 inches
Oil on canvas   33 x 15 cms
Painted circa 1935

PROVENANCE
Galerie Barbizon, Paris
St. George's Gallery, London
Seven Arts Ltd., London

André Dunoyer de Segonzac

LA MONTAGNE "SAN PE-I-RE" PRES GRIMAUX
(THE MOUNTAIN OF SAN PE-I-RE NEAR GRIMAUX)

Signed   29 x 36¼ inches
Watercolor   73.5 x 92 cms
Executed in 1957

Raoul Dufy (1877-1953)

It is sometimes difficult to explain Dufy's popularity among serious collectors of twentieth-century painting. That this popularity exists cannot be denied and the answer to the implied question "why?" must be that his work strikes a responsive chord and is universally appealing to a great number of sensitive, intellectual people. His seemingly simplistic style is derived from the radical innovations of the fauve movement and his calligraphic handling of line coupled with a marvelous ability to handle broad areas of color is especially suitable to his preferred súbject matter—the playgrounds of the rich and famous. All the sparkle and glamour of Monte Carlo, Nice, Ascot, and Deauville are captured in his glowing depictions of the pleasure capitals of the civilized world.

LE DERBY A EPSOM

Signed, and dated Epsom, 1930   27¾ x 5¼ inches
Oil on canvas   70.5 x 13 cms

EXHIBITIONS
Los Angeles County Museum; and the San Francisco, California, Palace of the Legion of Honor, *The Gladys Lloyd Robinson and Edward G. Robinson Collection*, 1956–57, no. 20.

Georges Rouault (1871-1958)

Beginning his career as an apprentice to a stained-glass maker, Georges Rouault enrolled as a student at the Ecole des Beaux-Arts in 1890, where he had the good fortune to have Gustave Moreau as his teacher. Rouault and a fellow student, Henri Matisse, learned much from Moreau, and when he died in 1898, Rouault continued to pursue his artistic career while at the same time serving as the first curator of the Musée Gustave Moreau in Paris. Kings, clowns, prostitutes, and judges, as the archetypal players in the comédie humaine, were treated again and again to Rouault's penetrating gaze and the paintings—with their rich, deep tones of primary color separated by heavy, dark outlines—echo his early training. Perhaps they are, for us, the stained-glass windows of our secular, contemporary cathedral which we call the modern world.

LE PIERROT (THE CLOWN)

Signed   26 x 20¼ inches
Oil on canvas   66.5 x 51.5 cms
Painted circa 1937–39

NOTE
"The Clown—we are all clowns—you—me, all of us who wear his mask." (From *Georges Rouault*, Galerie Beyeler catalogue of exhibition, 1962.)

EXHIBITIONS
Los Angeles County Museum; and the San Francisco, California, Palace of the Legion of Honor, *The Gladys Lloyd Robinson and Edward G. Robinson Collection*, 1956–57, no. 57.

Georges Rouault

POTENTATE

Oil on canvas   31¾ x 25½ inches
Painted circa 1937   81 x 65 cms

PROVENANCE
Ambroise Vollard, Paris
Galerie Jacques Seligman, New York

LITERATURE
Lionelle Venturi, *Georges Rouault*, 1948, p. 131, pl. 107, illus.

Georges Rouault

PAYSAGE (LANDSCAPE)

Signed   8 x 13 inches
Oil on canvas   20 x 33 cms
Painted circa 1937–38

PROVENANCE
André Weil, Paris

(detail)

Georges Rouault

PIERROT

Signed   9½ x 9 inches
Oil on canvas   24 x 23 cms
Painted circa 1937–39

PROVENANCE
Ambroise Vollard, Paris

83

Georges Rouault

LE TRIBUNAL DE PROVINCE (JUGES) (THE PROVINCIAL COURT)

Signed 25¾ x 40 inches
Oil on canvas 65.5 x 101.5 cms
Painted in 1938

PROVENANCE
Ambroise Vollard
Collection Madame de Galea
Sam Solz, New York

EXHIBITIONS
New York, Museum of Modern Art, *Forty Paintings from the Edward G. Robinson Collection,* 1953, no. 29.
Los Angeles County Museum; and the San Francisco, California, Palace of the Legion of Honor, *The Gladys Lloyd Robinson and Edward G. Robinson Collection,* 1956–57, no. 58, illus. in cat.

LITERATURE
Lionello Venturi, *Georges Rouault,* 1948, p. 67, illus.
Pierre Courthion, *Georges Rouault,* Catalogue Raisonné, 1961, p. 437, no. 349, illus

Georges Braque (1882-1963)

Braque was one year Picasso's junior, and so his career coincided with the Spanish master's for a few brief years in the second decade of the twentieth century when together they invented and developed Cubism. Prior to that, Braque had been briefly associated with the group known as fauves *(wild beasts) and after the cubistic experiment had been explored to its fullest, the two artists parted ways. In his later years Braque continued to develop his variations on the simple themes of still life and nude, always guided by an infallible sense of good taste and a deep awareness of the classical and formal traditions of French painting and culture.*

LE SAUCISSON

Signed	9½ x 13¾ inches
Oil on canvas	73 x 92 cms
Painted circa 1943	

NOTE
"Until the late '30s Braque's interiors had invariably contained a cluster of images centrally placed. Any sense of the room's volume had been created by taking 'measurements' from this hub of images. Now Braque has abandoned this hub and dispersed his still-life objects freely across the canvas. He suggests the volume of a room by a different approach, by means of a series of flat planes arranged without perspective. The position of these planes on the canvas, and the weight of color given to each, now determines the distance of objects from the eyes as well as their distance from one another." (Edwin Mullins, *The Art of Georges Braque*, 1968, p. 145.)

PROVENANCE
Paul Rosenberg & Co., New York
Georges Lurcy, New York, (sale: Parke-Bernet, Nov. 7, 1957, no. 11, illus. in cat.)

LITERATURE
Galerie Maeght, *Catalogue de l'Oeuvre de Georges Braque, Peintures 1942–47*, 1960, p. 52 illus.

EXHIBITIONS
New York, Paul Rosenberg Galleries, *Paintings by Braque, 1924–52*, 1952, no. 19 in cat.

Head of Balzac, by Rodin

Oceanic bowl, from Admiralty Island

Head, Pahouin,
from the Belgian Congo

Standing figure from Ivory Coast

Degas bronze dancer

89

SOME NOTES ON A HUSBAND

by JANE ROBINSON

Years ago, before I knew my husband, I went to a one-man show in an art gallery on Fifty-seventh Street (that was before Madison Avenue took over) and I was fascinated by a description of the artist's work in the catalogue. It revealed him "as a foe of simultaneity, but with an astonishing awareness of now, with remnants of then, combined with a luminosity which, while non-luminous, reveals an inner socio-political illumination, that is, at once, forward-looking and nostalgic. . . . He is a craftsman denying his craft and reveling in it."

E.G.R.'s mother Sara

E.G.R.'s grammar
school graduation picture

Well, I had a look. Simultaneity I thought I saw—but how it was possible to be luminous and non-luminous at the same time escaped me. I thought I detected some sort of socio-political imagery in the gray glob on the side of one canvas—but what kind of socio-political imagery I could not possibly say. And where, in the name of heaven, was he denying his craft and reveling in it? The fault, I knew, was mine. The description in the catalogue made me feel uninformed and successfully turned me off—I thought I'd better give up gallery-going, as pictures were clearly not my cup of tea.

Naturally, I married a collector, and shared a home and a life with him and his friends, the Messieurs Monet, Rouault, Pissarro, Modigliani, Vuillard, et al. Before my marriage, I knew nothing of art. Oh, I could gurgle the proper gurgles, oh the proper ohs, and murmur the proper murmurs, but I never really saw a picture until, by a process that was not entirely osmotic, Eddie taught me how to look. He has been patient. I had such a long way to go. When I first looked at his Modigliani with its long neck and one-sided tilt, what I saw was a man with a long neck and a one-sided tilt. I had no insight whatever into the artist's intention. And scarred as I was by my encounters with art catalogues and art criticism, I could find little help in reading about pictures. A moment of joy came when I discovered that Eddie had difficulty in reading about them too. We have an extensive library of art books but Eddie rarely consults the texts.

What Eddie has taught me is that, if you really want to learn, you must spend endless hours looking at the range of the artist. The best way to judge the artist's work is by the artist's own standards. Once you have steeped yourself in an artist's work, you will learn what it is that troubles him and what he says most forcefully, fluently, and beautifully.

93

Retrospective shows can destroy or build an artist for you. While talent is apparent at a glance, technique is not and should not be instantly visible. And sometimes talent and technique are indivisible.

I used to think that a white object was painted with white. Not so; it is rarely pure white; it is a dark color next to a lighter color that makes it appear this way. Impressionism is color next to color, one of the basic principles being a cool color next to a warm one. Did you ever try taking out a tiny bit of color in a painting and see how the canvas loses a great deal of its impact? Try putting one hand over a strong, dominant part of a picture and see for yourself.

The first time Eddie showed me this was in a painting by Courbet. We held our hands out to obliterate a touch of red and the canvas seemed flat. How marvelous to know just where to place a color! A canvas must hold in composition and color. Have you ever noticed how yellow the sky is at the horizon? The sky is not blue; it is a combination of red, yellow, mauve, lots of green, white, gray and blue, and any other color you like. There is no law.

It took me a long time to grasp the concept that everything is contained in and surrounded by light and air. Eddie has also taught me that Impressionist painters never use a straight line. They create the illusion by using short, uneven strokes of many colors.

I found out little by little that Eddie enjoys a picture without a scorecard, much the way he enjoys a piece of music or a fine bit of acting. With him it's ninety percent feeling. If the artist is doing a good job, he is carried along by him. He doesn't feel

E.G.R. in Navy during First World War

the need to analyze his work, as others do, in order to enjoy it. When I came to realize that you don't have to have some expert tell you how fine pictures are in order to experience an emotional reaction, I lost my self-consciousness. Overintellectualizing the arts, seeking hidden meanings can, I discovered, kill, or at least chill, your pleasure in them.

Unlike Eddie, I have no basic intuition about art, but constant exposure to great pictures has taught me not merely to look, but to see. I have learned that intent and motive in the artist are what to search for; I've come to know that the aesthetic experience is a merging between the artist and the viewer—and day by day, year by year, Eddie has subconsciously sharpened my thinking and my eyes so that I now see what I never thought it possible to see. This was not deliberate on his part; he never sought to be a teacher, or an explainer, or a guide; he simply shared his enthusiasm with me. And thus, he communicated to me his own love for and friendship with paint and canvas and genius. I hope I can communicate some part of it—minuscule though it may be.

Mine, of course, has been a unique role; I am the wife of a man who collects

94

pictures, though I must hasten to add that Eddie, not out of humility, doesn't consider himself a Collector. As a matter of fact, he doesn't consider himself a collector; he is simply a man who loves art and who, from the very first of his life, has found happiness when he is surrounded by it.

I have learned that many people ask embarrassing questions about my husband. It isn't only that they want to know if he's as tough off screen as he is on (he is not), but they bluntly ask, "Is Edward G. Robinson sincere about his love of art? Or is it just publicity—something worked up by his press agents?" Having been married to him for many years, I no longer bristle at this accusation; I can only say that the record denies it. Eddie doesn't even bother to do that; the private man ignores the inevitable suspicion of the public man. The private man is no different from any other who has an avocation different from the major thrust of his life. Eddie collects pictures; a lot of others collect rocks, or shells, or thimbles; we have a friend who systematically collects pipes and I knew a lady who was passionate about beer steins. The instinct of the collector is common in our society. In my husband—and now in me—it is both a dread disease and a love affair. Eddie said to me once: "Yes, a love affair and a rewarding one, even if it takes over your house, your family, your income, and your life. In time it becomes like the drug habit, you cannot live without it. Your walls may be bulging with paintings, business may be bad and prospects none too good; baby needs a pair of shoes; and you've sworn off buying. But you make an exception— just once—and there's nothing you can do about it. You just have to have the picture. There's no cure for it. Fact is you

E.G.R.'s collections— pipes, cigars, canes

don't want to be cured; you talk about stopping buying, but it's like Mark Twain talking about quitting smoking. 'I've done it hundreds of times,' he said. Well, so have I."

And hundreds of times, as I've looked around at the pictures on our walls, I've asked myself, where did it all start? How did it all begin? By what process did a struggling young actor like my husband come to use his lunch money for his first picture when he was nineteen years old? How did he know what to buy? In art, he is self-educated, but underneath his considerable layers of education there is the essential man whose knowledge of art is in his marrow. Still, I plagued him with my foolish question: Who taught you? His answer: "Looking taught me."

And so, at nineteen, he looked and bought an oil painting of a cow, a brown cow reclining in a meadow (called, believe it or not, *Reclining*), by an artist whose signature has long since become illegible. The brown cow lived with Eddie for half a century, and then somebody appropriated it, somebody who believed that any picture owned by us was automatically valuable.

95

This one was indeed valuable—even though it had cost him only a few dollars; he was living, as all actors did then and do now, in that inescapable uncertainty of not knowing when the play would close. And if it did close, what other job would there be? That is the Eddie I know—he buys pictures he loves, certainly not for investment or profit, nor as a hedge against inflation. And what does he love? Pictures that appeal to his emotions. Some of the artists he admires today, he had doubts about on first viewing.

Gallery connected
to the house

Eddie buys paintings out of instant enthusiasm. Five years ago we visited a major gallery and three Impressionist paintings caught his eye, a magnificent Monet, a great Vuillard, and a superb pastel by Degas. In twenty minutes he agreed to purchase all three; the blood had rushed to his head and he knew he must have them. He consults no one, certainly never his accountant. Consequently, we are always in debt to art dealers. And always will be, I suppose and hope.

It's not only the pictures in our house that Eddie cares about, it's the pictures in every collection and every museum the world over. To be married to Eddie is to be perpetually unable to buy a pair of fashionable shoes; I have museum feet, and a large collection of sensible shoes.

It seems to me we have been almost everywhere. Eddie has even accepted inferior parts in motion pictures provided they were made in some obscure corner of the world. Together we have seen the museums, private collections, and flea markets in Sweden, Norway, Greece, Turkey, Finland, Ireland, Spain, Africa, Japan, Hong Kong, and Cambodia, as well as in Chicago, Dallas, and every other major and many minor American cities. We even tried Egypt because Eddie was eager to see the royal antiquities. We went to the Cairo airport and reached the immigration shed, but were warned that our next stop would be an Egyptian jail. It was a pity, because the sphinx and Eddie would have been good friends; they have a lot in common. Neither of them ever says much.

As Eddie is instantly recognizable, visiting museums sometimes presents a problem for us—he has a whole new and young breed of fans since television. He likes the kids and refuses to talk to them about the good old days at Warner Brothers; he talks to them about the way art represents the best in man and how art is aspiration. Since aspiration is what kids seek, there is no generation gap between Eddie and the young. The real gap for him is with people who greedily think of art as an investment.

"Who," they ask him, "is the artist of the future? Which picture shall we buy that will be worth more tomorrow? Are pop and op art a good thing? Worth investing in? What about movable art, touchable art, mechanical art?" No answer from Eddie. He is both amused and bemused. This is what he feels:

The love of a picture is so personal that you must do your own thing; you are as good a critic as the next man. Your instinct may lead you to buy a picture for fifty dollars that in ten years will be worth more. Or, conversely, you may buy a picture for fifty dollars that in ten years will be worth nothing.

Once, in an interview, Eddie said, "So many people assume that when you collect art you are going in for 'culture,' for something special, something not everybody can appreciate. Well, I just can't conceive of art as special. I happen to love the works that artists create—pictures, poems, music—I love them as some people care for fine food, beautiful surroundings, or blondes. Through great paintings I met some of the finest human beings who ever lived—artists of genius. Through their beautiful works they come as near to achieving immortality as it is possible for people to do on this earth."

People ask me why Eddie prefers to collect the Impressionists and Post-Impressionists. Does this mean that he doesn't like or doesn't want the great classic masters, or the moderns? His answer was typical: "I don't buy the great classics, the Rembrandts, the Frans Halses, the

Studio, third floor
of the house

Rubenses, for a very simple reason: I can't afford them. Art is simply a matter of one's own choice and possibly pocketbook. Buy what you like."

I shall try to explain to you what our pictures mean to Eddie.

When he has a bad moment, the paintings comfort him; he goes from room to room, turning on lights and looking at the pictures alone and late at night. "Can't you see," Eddie once said to me, "that if you look at a Renoir canvas, all drenched in beautiful, sunshiny colors, then look out of your own windows at your own fields and streets and gardens, you see them with new eyes? That is what great painting is, that's what it's all about! Fine music makes the sounds of the rain and the wind and the swish of grain and the cries of hawkers in the streets have new meaning. It sweetens your ears and makes the experience of life a more exciting adventure. Fine painting makes the experience of life a glorious pageant that is always going on. It sensitizes your vision, it warms and enriches the soul. Imagine a nation of people made aware, through daily experience with the arts, of the glorious possibilities of life. It isn't a matter of educating them to something special or putting them through dull courses in the history of art. That's not the way to teach. I would like to see museums and art collectors band together to make art available to the millions of people in all lands. I firmly believe it could be done and that it would pay an incalculable spiritual dividend. Great paintings are windows which open for us the beautiful prospect of the world in which we live."

We live in a wonderful house, so wonderful that Eddie has paid for it three times. He bought it in 1933, the year his son was born; at the same time he started buying paintings. In a short while there was not enough wall space for hanging them. He commissioned Sam Marx, the great Chicago architect, to remedy the situation and together they worked out the plans, boarding windows to accommodate Degas's famous lady, *La Grande Danseuse*, and, finally, building the art gallery adjacent to our house. Fortunately, it was completed one month prior to the Second World War. Redoing it was more costly then the original purchase of the house and the lot. The last, and I hope final, purchase was at the time of Eddie's divorce from his first wife. It was part of the settlement.

Toscanini and E.G.R.

At the time of my husband's divorce, one of the stipulations of settlement was the sale of his entire collection of paintings. The California Statutes consider everything owned by husband and wife as community property and, when divorce occurs, the wife gets the double boiler, the husband gets his favorite ashtray, and the wife has the pick of the dishes. The great paintings in his former collection were:

Pierre Bonnard's *Street Scene, Paris; Woman Seated in a Studio; After the Bath; Still Life with Fruit*
Louis Eugène Boudin's *Beach Scene; Beach Scene*
Paul Cézanne's *The Black Clock*
Marc Chagall's *Rabbi with Torah*
Jean-Baptiste Camille Corot's *L'Italienne*
Edgar Degas's *Dancer Leaving Her Dressing Room; Two Dancers Resting; Dancers in Green; Dancers in Pink; La Grande Danseuse*
Eugene Delacroix's *Odalisque*
André Derain's *La Jolie Modèle*
Charles Dufresne's *Still Life with Chrysanthemums*
Raoul Dufy's *Epsom Derby*
Jean Louis Forain's *Court Room Scene*
Paul Gauguin's *Tahitian Flowers; Horsemen on the Beach*
Jean-Louis Géricault's *Mounted Trumpeter*
Vincent Van Gogh's *Portrait of Père Tanguy; Country Road, Arles*
Edward Hopper's *Street Scene, Gloucester*
Yasuo Kuniyoshi's *Daily News*
Henri Matisse's *The Dinner Table (La Desserte)*
Amadeo Modigliani's *The Zouave; Portrait of a Woman*
Claude Monet's *The Fourteenth of July; The Willows; Snow Landscape*
Berthe Morisot's *Before the Theatre*
Jules Pascin's *Nude with Green Hat*

Pablo Picasso's *Entombment*

Horace Pippin's *Christmas Morning*

Camille Pissarro's *Portrait of the Artist's Son, Georges; The Dead Tree; Boulevard des Italiens, Afternoon; La Rue Saint-Honoré; Le Pont Neuf*

Maurice Prendergast's *New England Harbor*

Pierre Auguste Renoir's *Girl with Red Plumed Hat; Place de la Trinité; Girl in Pink; Landscape; After the Bath*

Georges Rouault's *Nude; Head of a Woman; Two Peasants; The Old Clown; The Vase of Flowers; Christ of the Suburbs; Le Pierrot; Provincial Court Room Scene*

André Dunoyer de Segonzac's *Reclining Nude*

Georges Seurat's *Le Crotoy*

Walter Richard Sickert's *Study for Ennui*

Alfred Sisley's *Le Pont de Saint-Cloud*

Chaim Soutine's *The Communicant*

Eugene Speicher's *Portrait of a Welsh Girl*

Henri de Toulouse-Lautrec's *Portrait of Cipa Godebski*

Maurice Utrillo's *Cathedral of Notre Dame; Church of St. Medard; Street Scene, Scanes*

Edouard Vuillard's *Still Life with Oranges; The Artist's Mother at the Breakfast Table; Interior Scene*

Grant Wood's *Daughters of Revolution*

The loss of this collection was a tragedy to Eddie, but little by little, we purchased a second collection. However, he's never been able to buy back Georges Rouault's *The Old Clown.* To Eddie this painting represents the quintessence of "every man." For a time it was on loan to a Paris museum; when we saw it there, Eddie wept.

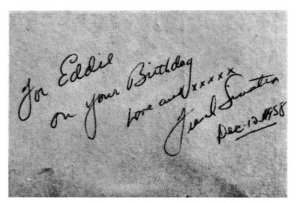

Constantin Guys painting, birthday gift from Frank Sinatra to E.G.R. with inscription

Collecting pictures is Eddie's hobby, but his paramount interest is acting, and though he says he is now in the twilight of his career, this is not true. He continues to work at his profession and continues to be in demand. The work invigorates him and the calling makes him proud. His gifts have matured and multiplied. I think that the reason he is still a star in his seventies is that his nonmoving pictures, even after a long day of shooting, refresh him. When he returns home he studies his lines and looks at a Monet.

If you think of movie stars in terms of wild parties around a swimming pool, don't come to our house. In the first place, we don't have a swimming pool; in the second, our parties grow wild only when we discuss not the odd things that have happened to the motion picture industry, but politics, pollution, and all the other concerns of responsible citizens. And, always, the pictures look down on the arguments and somehow manage to make our guests keep their voices lower.

Sometimes, when we have a party, two or three people wander throughout the house looking at the paintings. The only place that is off limits is a room on

Foyer, stairs, and living room of the house

the second floor, Eddie's. It does not contain guns. For Edward G. Robinson, who massacred people in *Little Caesar* and four other gangster pictures, guns are infinite terror. Mervyn Le Roy, who directed Eddie in *Little Caesar,* told me that, on the day when the scene called for Eddie to shoot, our big, brave gangster closed his eyes, and the scene had to be redone fifteen times until he could keep his eyes open.

So there are no guns but there are books; walls and walls of them. With apologies to Roth, Mailer, Updike, and Bellow, there are no novels. This is because, as an actor, Eddie *plays* fiction, plays parts in a make-believe world; and so, when he reads, he prefers biography, politics, and social comment. What he likes best are books about philosophy and linguistics that go to the root of language. For Eddie is no McLuhan; he worships words as he worships paint and music.

There are pictures in his room of his son, his granddaughter, and of his best friends. One he particularly likes is a lithograph of Sam Jaffe done by Mrs. Jaffe. There are autographed pictures of four or five presidents—most of them Democrats—and there is one of the British Royal Family with Eddie, superb in white tie, being presented to Their Majesties in 1963. The remarkable thing about that dress suit is that he had it made in London some thirty years before—it still fits him and he wears it frequently.

The furniture in the room consists of castoffs of various redecorations of our house; his favorite chair dates from his bachelor days and is still covered in the original material. Eddie doesn't like change.

On the old tables are mementoes of his life—bound movie scripts, scripts from his radio show *Big Town,* and shell casings from the Normandy Beach—and ashtrays, because Eddie smokes continually. He is one of the big cigar people of the world.

On the walls there are oils and watercolors. Not Picassos, or Matisses, or Segonzacs. They are pictures that Eddie has painted himself.

Eddie's birthday and Frank Sinatra's fall on the same day. They knew each other before they made a film together called *Hole in the Head,* but that picture

100

cemented their relationship. Their backgrounds were similar in a sense; they both came up the hard way. They both respected the art of acting and they both respected each other. And so, when during the filming of the picture, their birthday took place, the firm of Rogers and Cowan, public relations, gave them a party on a sound stage.

Frank sent Eddie a Constantin Guys drawing, which he had autographed on the back of the canvas. The framed drawing was beautifully tied with a bright red ribbon and delivered to our house. A week or so before, Sinatra had a party at his home and Eddie said to him that he thought it charming. So imagine our surprise when we received it.

Viewing paintings
in London

Eddie was embarrassed; he's not a "happy receiver"; we were both at a loss and could not reciprocate a gift of this magnitude. Frank, however, was nice enough to settle our predicament. He wished something personal from Eddie, something that money could not buy, he wanted one of Eddie's self-portraits. Eddie gave it to him with pleasure. It is the only painting by Edward G. Robinson that is in the hands of anybody but Edward G. Robinson. He does not really consider himself a painter. I do.

He is largely self-taught; he did take lessons for a while from Lorser Feitelson, the distinguished critic and painter, but even Mr. Feitelson found it difficult to come to the house at two in the morning. The fact is that Eddie is a nocturnal creature—he works from midnight to six in the morning, and this does present a problem in terms of models. That's why Eddie painted so many self-portraits; he could always be his own model. Two appear in this book.

It seemed to me that Eddie ought to have a catalogue of his collection and that it should include some of his own paintings. When I mentioned this casually at breakfast one morning, he almost threw me out of the house. At last he calmed down and he said, "The paintings in this house are not a collection any more but the remains of one." Then he looked at me with those soft, brown eyes. "As for me, Jane, you are not married to Rembrandt, you are married to an actor and a very bad Sunday painter." It was obvious that the catalogue was a dead issue.

One day Bill Harbach and his charming wife brought some people to the house; Eddie introduced me. "This gentleman," he said, "is Mr. Cass Canfield, of Harper & Row. He likes our paintings and feels that they would make an interesting book. I told him, dear, that was strictly your department and that he should talk to you."

I was surprised, because my husband, heretofore, had declined every publishing offer; my heart jumped. However, Mr. Canfield then proceeded to tell me about the headaches involved in producing a book of this kind. He said that

101

the pictures would have to be photographed by professional cameramen in our house and that proper lighting would be necessary as well as sufficient time. Accordingly, the best photographers were engaged and kept on call until such time as Eddie would be away. I knew he could not endure the picture-taking operation. Luckily, the time came when he agreed, as he always does, to go on a benefit tour for one of his favorite charities. We would surely be away ten days, which I knew would be too short a time because photography for fine art books is apt to take a minimum of six to eight months.

Royal Command
Performance, 1964

Our entire home became a gigantic photographic studio. I did not mention this to Eddie; I simply forgot to tell him, for I was certain that he would change his mind and refuse to permit it. To keep the whole matter secret, all equipment had to come through our back alley. I was very nervous; anything could happen. A foot through the Picasso? A coffee cup on a Rouault?

The color photography was finished in record time; no disaster had occurred. We were home again and Eddie was at work. Now came the hard part—getting into his room to photograph his own pictures. I take pride in including him among first-class contemporary painters; Eddie, most certainly, would not include himself, and when he reads this, it will be his first knowledge that his work is included. Heaven protect me.

This is not the first time I've asked Heaven to protect me from my own impulsiveness, a fault to which I plead guilty and one which, try as I will, I cannot overcome. While my husband is calm and logical, I am quick to anger, quick to joy, and agree to things which sometimes jeopardize my whole relationship with him. We have few differences of opinion except about matters of major importance, like whether or not he should have a beard and moustache (I prefer him clean-shaven and I've lost); whether he should wear blue or gray suits (he prefers blue and I prefer gray, so he wears blue); whether or not the eggplant is seasoned properly (I like a touch of garlic, he hates it. Result, no touch). And above all, whether or not he should appear on TV panel shows.

His answer to all appeals, requests, and offers is a resounding "No." My answer is, "Why not, dear? Why not?" Thereupon he gives me one of those chilling Jack Benny stares, followed instantly by an engaging Eddie Robinson grin. When you've been married as long as I have you know precisely what that means. Eddie does not want to continue the discussion. I think the reason that he invariably says "No" is partly due to his faulty hearing and his inability to ad lib. He's not a "stand-up comedian"; he is an actor whose lines are written for him. Yet he is a superb conversationalist.

When Johnny Carson's *Tonight* show was being taped on the West Coast the

102

producer made his usual inquiry, "Would Eddie appear?" His answer was "Thank you, no." The producer called and tried to persuade him once more; I answered the phone and committed him to the show. We began to plot what Eddie might do on the show. Inadvertently—was it subconscious or deliberate?—I mentioned that Eddie was a painter and asked whether it might be arranged that his own pictures be exhibited on the show? I knew I was treading on dangerous ground, but the more dangerous it got, the more intrigued I became. I became involved in a cloak and dagger conspiracy.

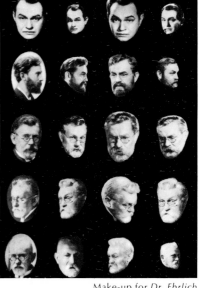

Make-up for *Dr. Ehrlich*

I began to steal original EGRs from our own home; I stealthily crept down the stairs, hoping that Eddie would not see me. My plan was to have the pictures framed and to show them on the program; also to get Eddie to the NBC Studios without his knowledge. The pay for this performance was two hundred sixty-five dollars; we could use the money. The *Tonight* show started me on the road to crime as Mrs. Little Caesar. To compound the felony, I decided to give a party the same night; it was to be my shield against his disapproval.

Having now involved myself in this plot, it was necessary to have co-conspirators. My partners in crime were Sam Jaffe, George Burns, Karl Malden, and Debbie Reynolds. One might say that we were the mob and Eddie the victim. I was nearly caught a thousand times; a carload of groceries delivered to our house wasn't easy to explain!

In all the years we had lived in California we had never been to the NBC Burbank Studios, where Eddie's paintings now were. Georgie Jessel had invited us there for a taping of his show, the night before Eddie was to appear. And because Eddie is devoted to George, he decided to go. There we were, Eddie, the paintings, and I.

Then came *the* day—I was prepared to be the second ex-Mrs. Edward G. I had sent my wedding ring to the scene of the crime; he was to return it if I was forgiven. The surprise worked. The audience loved Eddie; he loved them. Suddenly he was home again and returned the ring; all was forgiven. He enjoyed the party.

Alone and quietly the following evening, we watched the program. I particularly liked Eddie's reaction when his paintings came into view. I remember so well his comment on seeing his own work, "I realized, when I began painting myself, that I didn't pay enough for the pictures I purchased. But, my dear Jane, please remember in the future, I paint for my own pleasure. Let's keep it that way."

Eddie, in a rare moment, wrote something about his feeling for art:

"I sit there quietly and something passes between us—between these glorious living works of great artists and myself, who, for a brief while, am privileged to be

103

their custodian. Contemplating them at such moments, I am carried away by feeling that beyond this room, these shapes on the wall, stands the world they came from. It is not today a perfect world, and even now fires are burning at its edges. Men die, and slogans and powerful evil forces press us in. And when I think of the men who torment us and make turmoil in our lives, and then see and feel the men who made these paintings, I suddenly have a moment of hope. For, if man could make this beauty on my walls, if he could produce the life and form and color that make the magic of these canvases, there is hope for one's Earth, and for us."

Bookcase in E.G.R.'s room

PAINTINGS BY
EDWARD G. ROBINSON

E.G.R.'s first painting, circa 1951

Self-Portrait, 1962

Study of friend Sam Jaffe, 1957

Self-Portrait, 1964

The Black Clock by Cézanne, copied by E.G.R. in 1957

White Roses, circa 1958

Epilogue
EDWARD G. ROBINSON
ON COLLECTING ART

—From a speech given to the
American Booksellers Association,
June 1, 1971

As far as I know, this is the only book on art which has a plot.

My wife was the plotter. Along with many of my former friends. People came into my house and took away our paintings one by one. To freshen up the frames, I was told. Eventually I discovered they were being photographed. Insurance reasons, I was told.

The phone rang, night and day, and distinguished people I would have been glad to talk to about anything at all would insist on talking to my wife instead. Well, I thought to myself, I'm getting along in years and perhaps I've become a bore.

No, they were plotting, and planning, and printing, and publishing this book. Cass Canfield and his mob, all of them, my wife included, are worse gangsters than I ever was.

I snarled when I discovered what had been done, and my snarl has lost none of its venom down through the years. I seized the first copy when it came my way, and literally tore it apart, looking for mistakes—a blur in the printing, a false color somewhere, a false note in the text. Anything on which I could vent my rage. Unfortunately, I found nothing.

I hate to admit it, but it's a very good book. I'll probably buy more copies of it than anyone else, and wind up drinking more tea than any reasonable man could possibly want at afternoon sociables, discussing art—a thing I prefer leaving to critics.

I intend to be honest on such occasions, if only as an act of revenge. There is one error in the book which I will mention on every possible occasion. That error shall be made known.

It took me a while to find it, but it's there. I am referred to in the book as an art collector. I am not.

I have not collected art, art collected me. I never found a painting, they found me. I have never even *owned* a work of art, they own *me*. What people call my collection is this group of masterpieces that collected each other, and then very kindly allowed me to go into debt to pay the bills.

113

Of course, I started as a collector. A true collector. I can remember as if it were only yesterday the heart-pounding excitement as I spread out upon the floor of my bedroom The Edward G. Robinson Collection of Rare Cigar Bands. I didn't play at collecting. No cigar anywhere was safe from me. My father and uncles and all their friends turned their lungs black trying to satisfy my collector's zeal.

And then came cigarette cards, big-league baseball players. I was an insatiable fiend, and would cheerfully trade you three Indian Joes for one of that upstart newcomer, Ty Cobb.

When I got my first long pants, and sex reared its lovely head, I switched to those never-to-be-forgotten color cards of the soubrettes, the great and beautiful ladies of the stage and music halls, Lily Langtry, Lotta Crabtree, Lillian Russell, Bessie Barriscale—they don't have names like that anymore. Or chests either.

Ah yes, I remember well what it was like to be a true collector, that soft explosion in the heart, that thundering inner "yes" when you see something you must have or die. For over thirty years I made periodic visits to Renoir's *Luncheon of the Boating Party* in a Washington museum, and stood before that magnificent masterpiece hour after hour, day after day, plotting ways to steal it.

I'm glad I no longer feel that way, and I am not still a collector. I have sworn off. Again. And it gets easier each time. The first hundred times I swore off were very difficult, even painful. Now there's nothing to it, just a slight touch of heartburn is all.

As I have indicated, I no longer possess paintings, they possess *me*. That process began a long time ago, when, innocently enough, I played a gangster in a movie.

In a bewildering succession of nasty-tempered roles, I murdered many of my fellow actors, or was liquidated by them. I died in alleys, on street corners, in tawdry saloons, and was frequently conducted to a well-deserved and overcooked end in various sizzling electric chairs. In a word, I found that crime does pay.

One fine day, I spent more than I had paid for the house in which I lived, and brought home a fine painting and hung it on my wall. I had studied the work of the artist for many years and yearned for one touch of his greatness, and at last I had it.

Not long afterward, I brought home another painting, almost as fine, but not quite. The first painting refused to be in the same house with it. There ain't room enough for both of us, the painting told me, one of us has got to go and it ain't going to be me.

So I went into debt, the first of many times, to provide a suitable companion for that tyrannical first. And then the two of them ganged up on me when I brought home a third. Not good enough they told me in no uncertain terms. Not half good enough. Great paintings are like that. They choose their own company, and they can be very particular, very demanding, as they collect each other, and their victim, *me*.

And so it was that I became the collected, instead of a collector. They made me change the shape of the house, the walls, the drapes, the carpets—even the furniture had to be something of which they would gently approve.

In time they forced me to buy the lot next door and add on a small gallery and then, of course, they began to invite their own guests—students, artists, curators, art lovers, even glib museum officials who praised the paintings and offered to borrow them permanently—at no cost to me whatever, mind you, except for the empty walls they would leave behind. They even had thoughtful plans for how I could write off the paintings, providing, of course, that I would get written off first. And somehow they gave me the impression part of the deal would be for me to hurry up about that.

One way or another, the guest list grew larger and larger. Whole groups would show up, with a lecturer. When, as sometimes still happens, the lecturer does not appear, I find myself introducing these benevolent despots to their visitors, or my wife conducts the tour, while I sneak up the back stairs of my own house so as not to detract attention from the paintings. Even our houseman has caught the fever, and has become quite expert, until it now seems indecent to ask such an eminent commentator on line and color to serve the evening roast.

Now this collection of paintings has reached what I daresay was their ultimate goal. They have collected themselves into a book.

It was time for that. The explosion of art books throughout the world, the rocketing attendance in museums everywhere, have made art the best show in town, outdrawing every long-run play or big hit movie that was ever made.

Most of that interest, I like to think, is pure and very simple. The search for beauty that never ends. The quest for truth that inspires every great artist. The need to know the meaning of the world on which we find ourselves thrust toward a hidden and unknown destiny.

There is another aspect to this renaissance that I do not find either pure or pleasant, the usage of art for personal prestige. That charming little Utrillo that hangs over the fireplace so that the man who owns it can say, it is mine, and important, and therefore I am important. The inner eye and often tragic vision of these artists cannot be bought by any man, nor do their paintings really ever belong to merely one of us. If we are very fortunate, as I have been, we are allowed at most a lovely time of custody, no more.

People sometimes ask me, and others simply speculate—and either one of those things grates my few remaining teeth—what this collection is worth in dollars. I have no idea. Nor do I care.

However, I know what they cost, and there is no dollar sign in front of it. They cost all the years of my life, much of my capacity for love, and they demand my presence, my thoughts, my inner heart. In exchange, all they permit me is to live among them for a little while.

They have a unity among themselves, as any keen eye will soon discover, warmth and color and deep emotion, with the hand of the artist strongly evident. Usually that hand is sunburnt, careless of weather, oblivious to pain. Always there is the inner eye, the search for a fragment of truth, the mystery of living, and the meaning of time.

There is music in them, laughter in some and tears in others, clean air and foul, and most of them convey, to me at least, a sense of smell and sound. Even touch.

I touch them sometimes, with the flat of my hand very gently, amazed again and ever again that little tubes of long-dried pigment could be arranged in such lovely order, that an instant of times gone by, people long dead, music faded away, eyes long ago dimmed and empty, could suddenly be alive once more and very real—breathing deep and slow and forever.

Sometimes late at night, when the house is quiet, and the last guest has gone, I go into my living room and sit down among these quiet friends, and we study each other very gravely, and I hope with mutual pleasure.

Something passes between us, between these glorious living works that will exist forever, and I myself, who will not.

We found you in your youth, they tell me, and you served to bring us together. Soon enough we will scatter again, but we will not soon forget you, old friend.

Contemplating them at such moments, I am carried away by the deep and satisfying realization that beyond the room, past those intricate shapes upon the wall, still stands the world they came from. It is never a perfect world, and fires continually rage at the edges. Men die as the artists died, their subjects with them; new slogans are screamed at the sky, and powerful forces pull us this way and that between evil and good, with no man able to clearly say which is which.

But when I think of the stream of history that torments us endlessly, and makes turmoil in all our lives, I suddenly have a moment of hope. For if man himself, sometimes ravaged by drugs, by hunger, and by dissipation, mad with much heart—if man could make this beauty on my walls, if he could produce the life and form and color that make the magic of these canvases, and do it only from tinted earth, stirred with insight and passion and faith, why then there is hope for us all.

We too are made of earth.

ACKNOWLEDGMENTS
(In alphabetical order)

Cass Canfield, Sr.—My inspiration and co-conspirator—Senior Editor of
    Harper & Row
Sara Keast—Secretary to Mr. Canfield, Harper & Row
Randall MacDougall—Writer, Director, and President of the Writer's Guild,
    Los Angeles, California
Peter Mollman—Production Manager of Harper & Row
David Nash—Vice-President and Member of the Board of Directors, Parke-Bernet
    Galleries, New York City
Elizabeth Pendlebury—My invaluable assistant
Peregrine Pollen—President and Member of the Board of Directors of
    Parke-Bernet Galleries, New York City
Paul Rewald—Parke-Bernet Galleries, New York City
George Sidney—Producer-Director of Motion Pictures and Television, Beverly
    Hills, California
Mel Traxel—Photographer, Pacific Palisades, California
Pauline Weymouth—Executive Assistant to Mr. Sidney, Los Angeles, California

Their interest and enthusiasm made the entire project possible.